SMALL BUSTED WOMEN HAVE BIG HEARTS

By Herbert I. Kavet
Designed and Illustrated by Martin Riskin

AN Ivory Tower BOOK

Contemporary Books, Inc.
Chicago

Published by arrangement with Ivory Tower
    Publishing Company, Inc.
by Contemporary Books, Inc.
180 North Michigan Avenue, Chicago, Illinois 60601
Manufactured in the United States of America
International Standard Book Number: 0-8092-5353-4

INTRODUCTION

It's true; Small busted women do have to have big hearts. Their hearts grow big because of the male's childish obsession with mammoth mammaries. These obsessions force small busted women to develop more meaningful personalities; how else can they cope with the years of slights and teasing? You might ask, "If these hearts are so big, where do small busted women keep them?" They keep their big hearts within their compact and slim bodies, that are full of love and empathy and warmth.

With special thanks to the women at Ivory Tower, big busted and small (with some medium ones, too), who contributed most of the ideas for this tome.

SMALL BUSTED WOMEN

Don't have to worry about drooping. They always pass the "pencil" test.

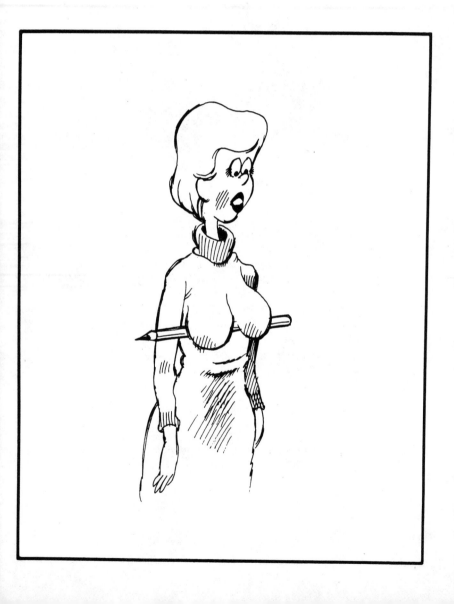

SMALL BUSTED WOMEN

Can go braless; it's comfortable in warm
weather and sexier the year-round.

SMALL BUSTED WOMEN

Never have trouble in turnstiles or revolving doors — even when carrying bundles.

SMALL BUSTED WOMEN

Fit into the teeniest bathing suits without looking overstuffed.

SMALL BUSTED WOMEN

Can wear tight sweaters without being embarrassed or without being the unwanted center of attention.
A Small Busted Woman who does want to be the center of attention can always wear tighter jeans or shorter skirts.

SMALL BUSTED WOMEN

Can sleep on their stomachs.

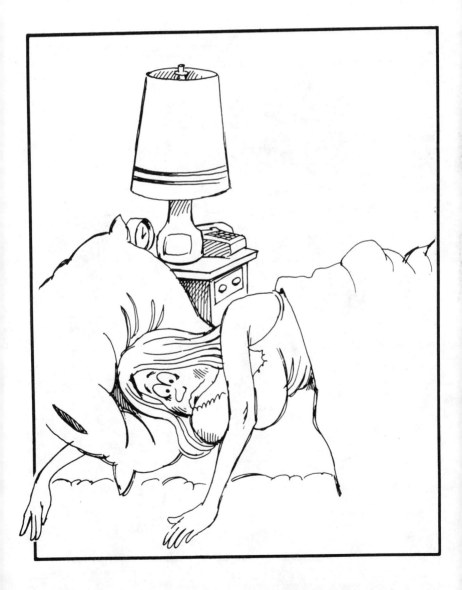

SMALL BUSTED WOMEN

Find it much easier to shop for clothes. They look better in a wider range of clothes, and never have to worry about hemline alterations.

SMALL BUSTED WOMEN

Are noticed for a lovely face. Men see their hair, their smile, their eyes.

SMALL BUSTED WOMEN

Are appreciated for themselves, their personalities, their abilities. Small Busted Women never have to wonder why they got the job.

SMALL BUSTED WOMEN

Always look younger.

SMALL BUSTED WOMEN

Can sunbathe topless on gay beaches.

SMALL BUSTED WOMEN

Sports is an area where the superiority of small busted women really becomes evident. Can you imagine a 16-year-old gymnast with bazooms like Dolly Parton's?

SMALL BUSTED WOMEN

Score much higher in diving competitions.
There simply is less splash.

SMALL BUSTED WOMEN

Can take an aerobic dance class without running the risk of knocking themselves out.

SMALL BUSTED WOMEN

Have the delightful experience of watching themselves grow when they get pregnant. Their big hearts do not shrink during this short experience with bigger boobs. In most cases, their hearts grow even bigger.

SMALL BUSTED WOMEN

Know that anything more than a handful
is wasted.

SMALL BUSTED WOMEN

Get much less hassle when passing construction sites.

SMALL BUSTED WOMEN

Make superior limbo dancers.

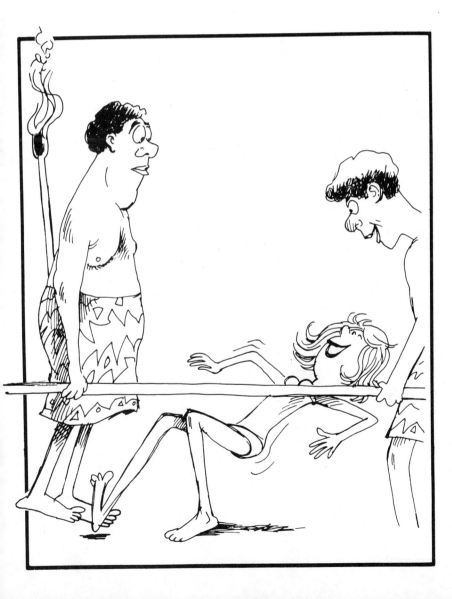

SMALL BUSTED WOMEN

Look much better in winter coats, and can easily wear layers of clothes.

SMALL BUSTED WOMEN

Won't cause an overflow if they are the last ones in the hot tub.

SMALL BUSTED WOMEN

Know that when someone touches them, it's because he (or she) loves them, and not only to fondle her curves.

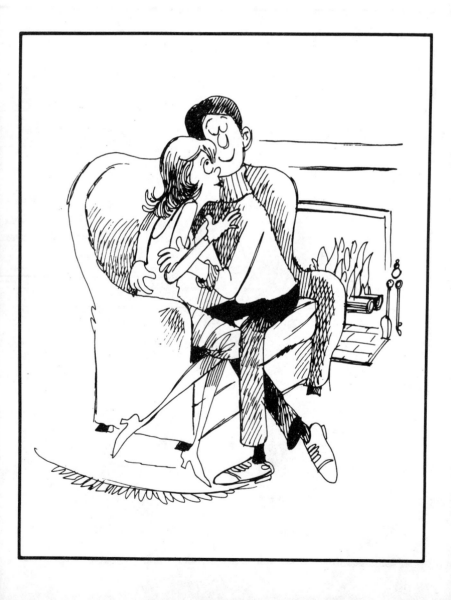

SMALL BUSTED WOMEN

Can dance cheek to cheek without throwing their partner's back out.

SMALL BUSTED WOMEN

Find that dribbled food makes it to the napkin on their lap.

SMALL BUSTED WOMEN

Know that people can read the entire message on their T-Shirts.

SMALL BUSTED WOMEN

Don't have to worry about buttons popping, or
not closing properly.

SMALL BUSTED WOMEN

Don't cause traffic accidents every time they bend over in public.

SMALL BUSTED WOMEN

Are much less embarrassed in tight spaces.

SMALL BUSTED WOMEN

Are in much less danger when having a corsage
pinned on them.

SMALL BUSTED WOMEN

Don't jiggle when jump-roping or running up stairs.

SMALL BUSTED WOMEN

Can dance with a shorter man without embarrassing him, or threatening his eyesight.

SMALL BUSTED WOMEN

Don't get the "nonchalant" elbows in crowds.

SMALL BUSTED WOMEN

Rarely pop out of low-cut gowns.

SMALL BUSTED WOMEN

Can always see their toes and shoes.

SMALL BUSTED WOMEN

Have no trouble sliding behind the wheel of small cars.

SMALL BUSTED WOMEN

Are much less threatening to other women. They make friends easier and are less selfish, which all contributes to the growth of their hearts.

SMALL BUSTED WOMEN

Usually find more standing room on public transportation.

SMALL BUSTED WOMEN

Seem to have fewer accidents.

SMALL BUSTED WOMEN

Can wear designer clothes.

SMALL BUSTED WOMEN

Have more erogenous zones. No kidding, their compact bodies tend to concentrate nerve endings, and small busted women definitely have more fun during sex.

SMALL BUSTED WOMEN

Aren't asked to be cheerleaders as often. Instead, they can snuggle comfortably with their boyfriends in the stands, and further develop their warm personalities.

SMALL BUSTED WOMEN

Can come late to a theater and not disrupt an entire aisle.

SMALL BUSTED WOMEN

Can hug closer and nicer and longer.

SMALL BUSTED WOMEN

Always look thinner.

SMALL BUSTED WOMEN

Attract men with a greater appreciation for intellect, beauty and personality.

SMALL BUSTED WOMEN

Can always find "bargains" in the teens' clothes department.

SMALL BUSTED WOMEN

Are more comfortable wearing seat belts.

SMALL BUSTED WOMEN

Can maneuver down the aisle on a crowded plane.

SMALL BUSTED WOMEN

Can participate in more jumping events at picnics and gyms.

SMALL BUSTED WOMEN

Always look fine in stripes.

SMALL BUSTED WOMEN

Don't always receive lingerie as gifts.

SMALL BUSTED WOMEN

Have less problems disguising themselves
at Halloween.

SMALL BUSTED WOMEN

Can save a fortune on their underwear.

SMALL BUSTED WOMEN

Take up lots less space.

SMALL BUSTED WOMEN

Never have "KNOCKERS". Knockers hang around street corners and go out with pimply teenage boys who take them to cheap amusement parks.

SMALL BUSTED WOMEN

Don't have to worry about the alligator being on the side of their shirt.

SMALL BUSTED WOMEN

Can play certain musical instruments with greater safety.

SMALL BUSTED WOMEN

Are never called "BIMBOS". Bimbos are not too bright, and while men love to get Bimbos into the back seat of cars, they seldom take them to meet their mothers.

SMALL BUSTED WOMEN

Can get closer to their men in cold weather.

SMALL BUSTED WOMEN

Can find things under beds.

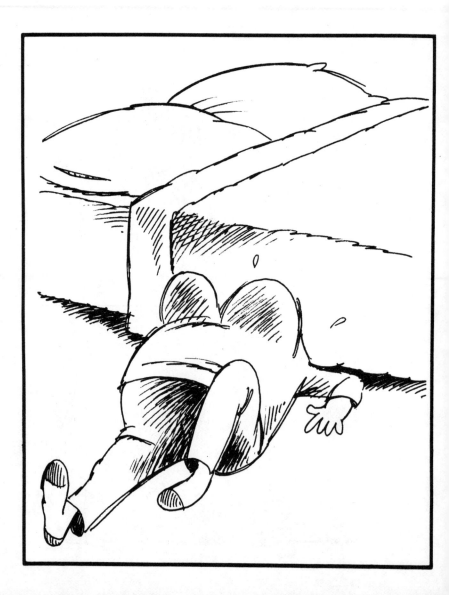

SMALL BUSTED WOMEN

Can be liberated enough to make their own car repairs.

SMALL BUSTED WOMEN

Are more sensual and sexy. They learn to use parts of their bodies that big busted women never think of.

SMALL BUSTED WOMEN

Can wear V-neck tops and men have to get very close to check them out.

SMALL BUSTED WOMEN

Can get into theaters, sporting and other events at children's rates.

SMALL BUSTED WOMEN

Never have their chests referred to as "BAZOOMS". Bazooms kind of sound like an aggressive appendage that is going to attack you, and small busted women never do that.

SMALL BUSTED WOMEN

Can squeeze through crowded places without knocking things over.

SMALL BUSTED WOMEN

Don't have to wear special sports bras
when exercising.

SMALL BUSTED WOMEN

Know that really good things come in small packages.

SMALL BUSTED WOMEN

Don't have their chests referred to as "MELONS". This confusion with supermarket fruit departments only leads to having the "melons" squeezed.

SMALL BUSTED WOMEN

Can pledge allegiance without someone leering or making a rude remark.

SMALL BUSTED WOMEN

Don't have to worry about getting the wrong tooth filled at the dentist.

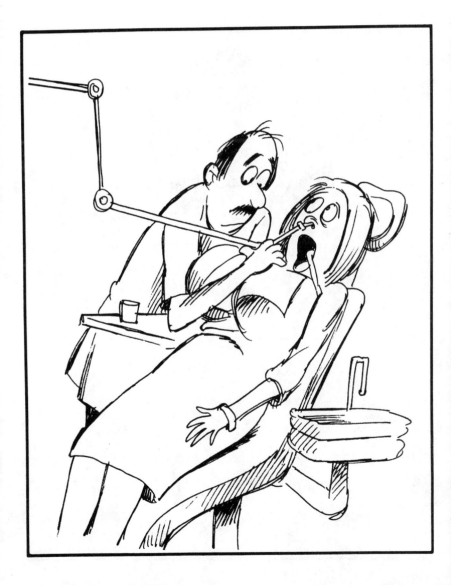

SMALL BUSTED WOMEN

Don't have "GLOBES". While this name could denote a certain worldliness, in fact it conjures up images of enormously round and fat flesh.

SMALL BUSTED WOMEN

Find they have more "eye contact"
in conversations.

SMALL BUSTED WOMEN

Don't have "HEADLIGHTS". They are not automobiles and their breasts aren't the first thing that comes into view in the distance.

SMALL BUSTED WOMEN

Can jog braless, probably without harassment.

SMALL BUSTED WOMEN

Mature into more elegant women.

SMALL BUSTED WOMEN

Don't have "MANACAS". No one knows what this somewhat Spanish sounding name refers to, but it doesn't sound flattering.

SMALL BUSTED WOMEN

Can borrow lovers' clothes and return them in the same condition.

SMALL BUSTED WOMEN

Can rarely threaten their friends' relationships.

SMALL BUSTED WOMEN

Don't have "KNOBS". Knobs are for touching and turning and, while perfect on radios and TV's, are not something Small Busted Women carry around.

SMALL BUSTED WOMEN

Make better archers.

SMALL BUSTED WOMEN

Are never "STACKED". There is no class, no elegance in being stacked. Being stacked sounds like a big pile of something.

SMALL BUSTED WOMEN

Can wear long necklaces without them getting caught or lost.

SMALL BUSTED WOMEN

Are more tolerant. They understand smallness and don't condemn size in others.

SMALL BUSTED WOMEN

Are much harder to hit in fencing competitions.

SMALL BUSTED WOMEN

Can always look a little bigger if they really want to.

SMALL BUSTED WOMEN

Find many exercises much more comfortable.

SMALL BUSTED WOMEN

Can close business deals with many less "strings" attached.

SMALL BUSTED WOMEN

Can wrap their arms all the way around their men.

SMALL BUSTED WOMEN

Don't blow their horn each time they squirm around in a compact car.

SMALL BUSTED WOMEN

Make great dancers (ballet) and carry themselves with more grace and rhythm.

SMALL BUSTED WOMEN

Have busts and bosoms. They have bodies and boobies and breasts and even bubbies and probably lots of other nice things to call their chests.

SMALL BUSTED WOMEN

Are often a little insecure because of the size of their figures. They overcome this with a more expansive personality and inner glow that many laymen describe as having a big heart.

These other humorous titles are available at fine bookstores or by sending $3.95 each plus $1.00 per book to cover postage and handling to the address below.

Please send me:

QUAN.		TITLE
	5352-6	Skinny People Are Dull and Crunchy Like Carrots
	5370-4	A Coloring Book for Pregnant Mothers to Be
	5367-4	Games You Can't Lose
	5358-5	The Trite Report
	5357-7	Happy Birthday Book
	5356-9	Adult Crossword Puzzles
	5359-3	Bridget's Workout Book
	5360-7	Picking Up Girls
	5368-2	Games for the John
	5340-2	Living in Sin
	5341-0	I Love You Even Tho' . . .
	5342-9	You Know You're Over 50 When . . .
	5363-1	You Know You're Over 40 When . .
	5361-5	Wimps
	5354-2	Sex Manual for People Over 30
	5353-4	Small Busted Women Have Big Hearts
	5369-0	Games You Can Play with Your Pussy Cat (and Lots of Other Stuff Cat Owners Should Know)
	5366-6	Calories Don't Count If You Eat Standing Up
	5365-8	Do Diapers Give You Leprosy? What Every Parent Should Know About Bringing Up Babies
	5355-0	I'd Rather Be 40 Than Pregnant
	5362-3	Afterplay: How to Get Rid of Your Partner After Sex

Send me _____ books at $3.95* each $_____

Illinois residents add 8% sales tax; California residents add 6% sales tax: _____

Add $1.00 per book for shipping/handling   _____

TOTAL $_____

☐ Check or M.O. payable to Best Publications

Charge my   ☐ Visa   ☐ MasterCard

Acct. #_____ Exp. Date ___/___

X_____

Signature (required only if charging to Bankcard)

Name _____

Address_____

City/State/Zip_____

*Prices subject to change without notice.

Best Publications, Department IT

180 N. Michigan Ave., Chicago, IL 60601   BB 0784